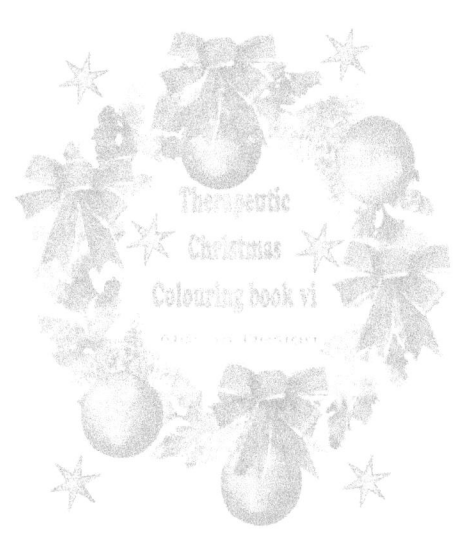

Therapeutic
Christmas
Colouring book vi

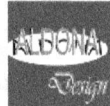

We would appreciate your Opinion
About this book by leaving a Review
link follows
www.amazon.com/author/aldonadesign

Email : **aldonadesign@gmail.com**
Instagram: https://www.instagram.com/aldona_design
Artwork:- http://www.redbubble.com/people/aldona

This Therapeutic
Christmas
Colouring book VI
Belongs to

_____

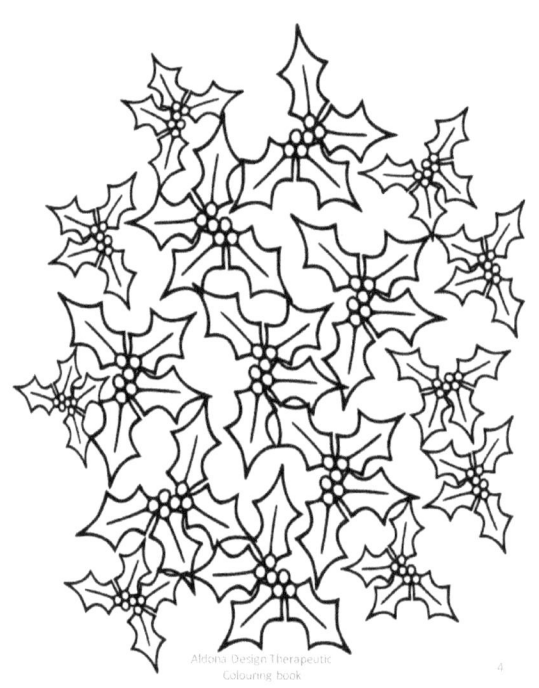

Holly Pattern page 4

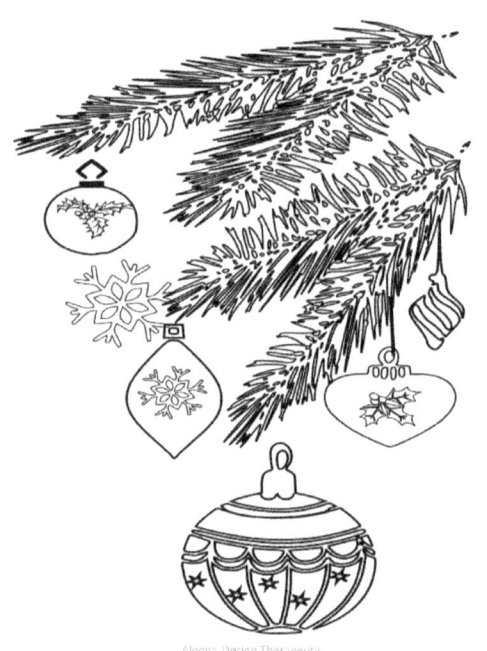

Ornaments page 6

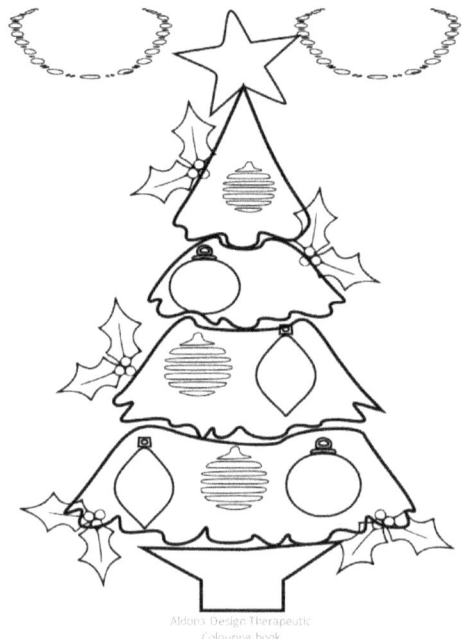

Christmas Tree page 8

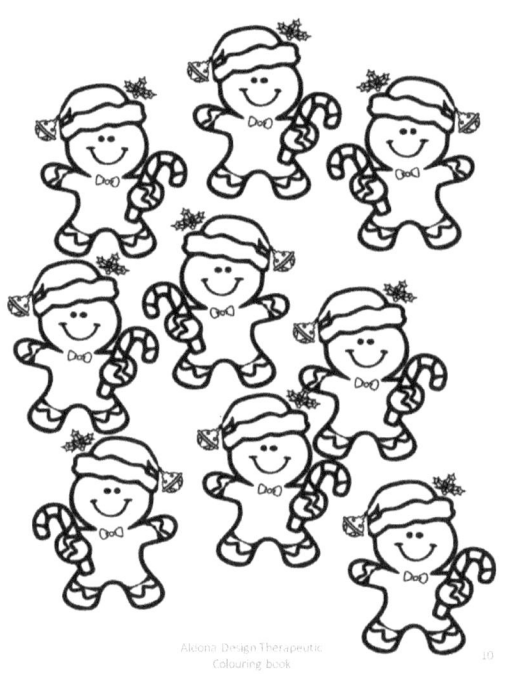

Gingerbread page 10

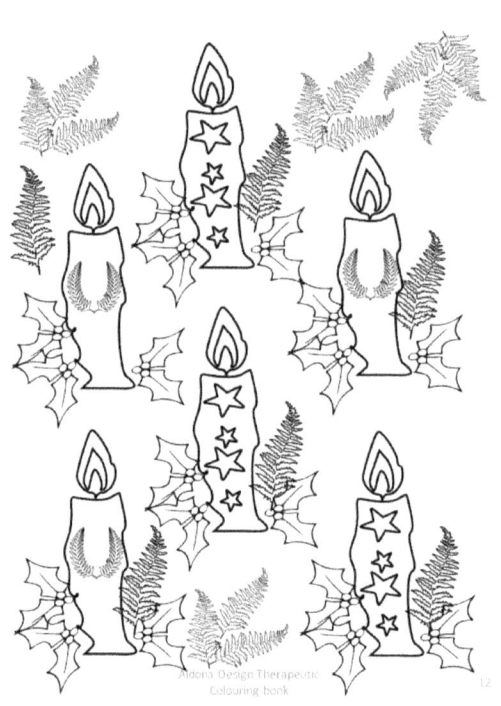

Candles page 12

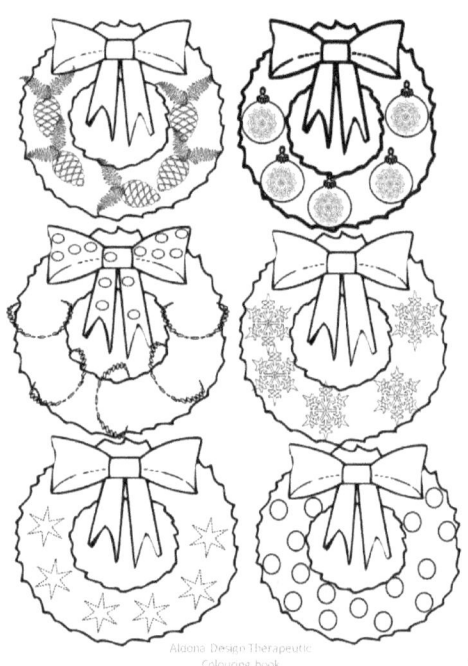

Wreaths page 14

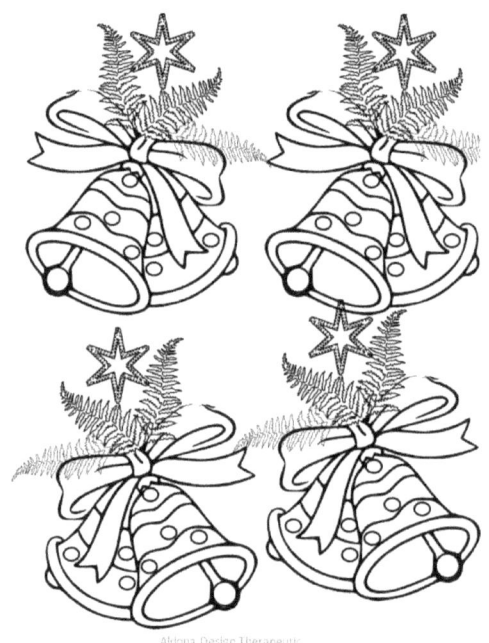

Bells page 16

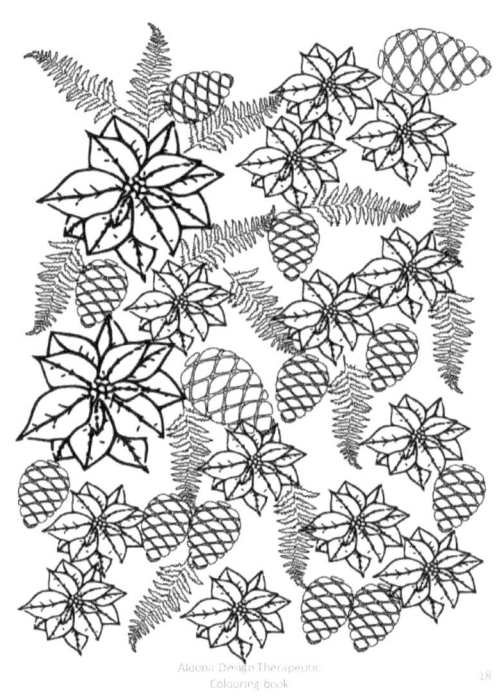

Poinsettia page 18

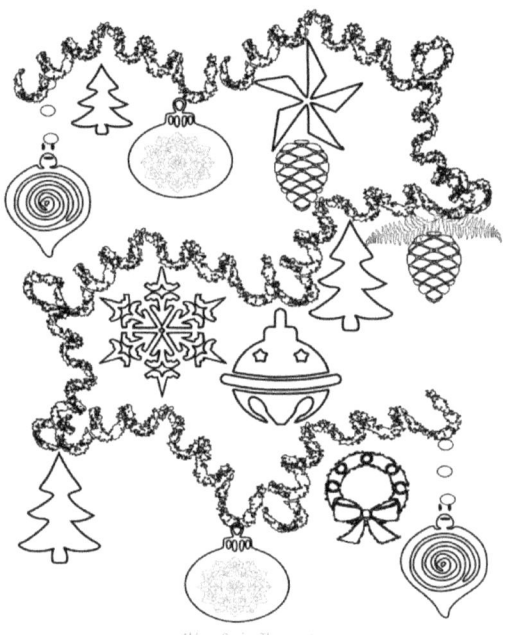

Streamers & Ornaments page 20

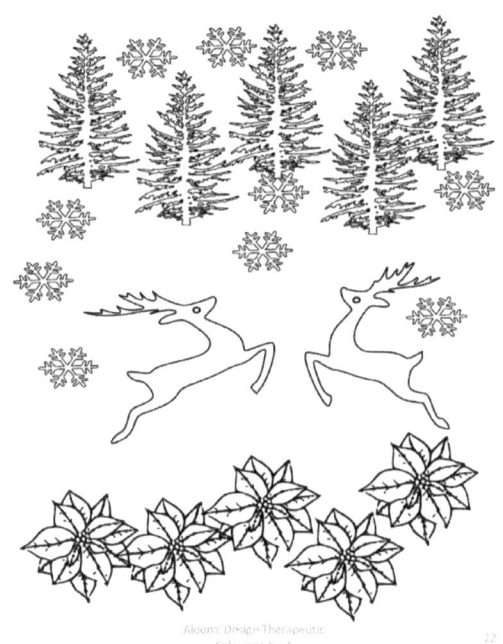

Reindeer & Trees page 22

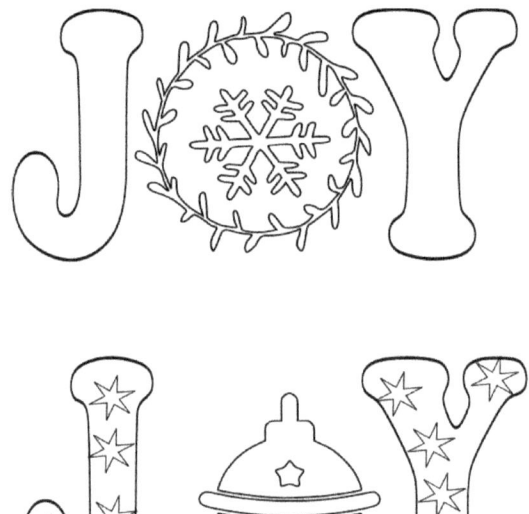

Joy page 24

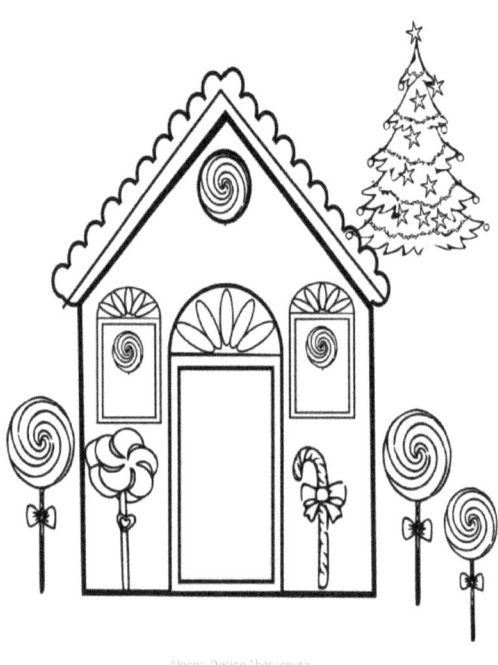

Gingerbread house page 26

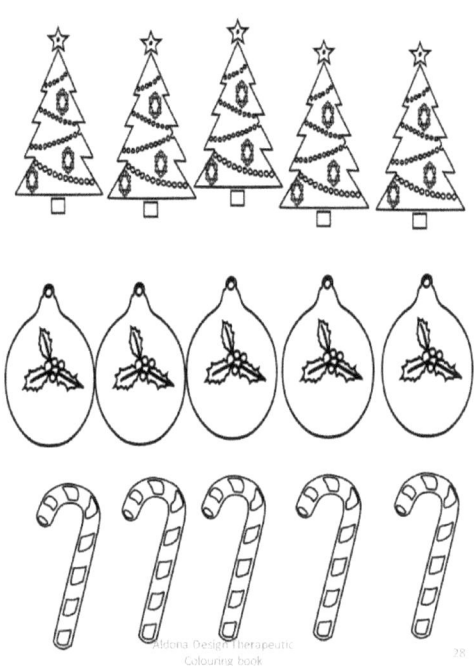

Ornaments page 28

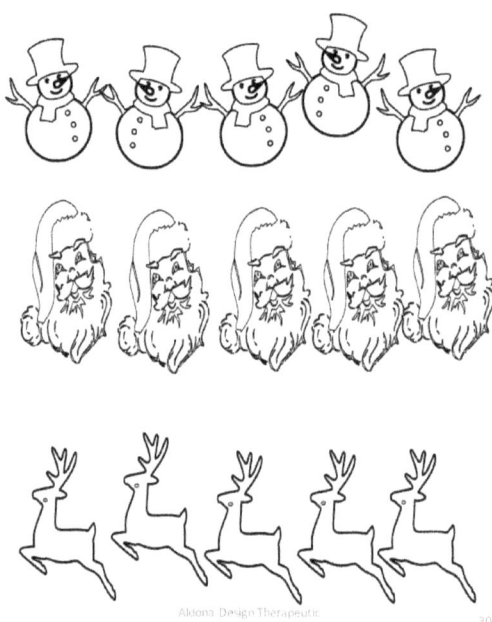

Ornaments page 30

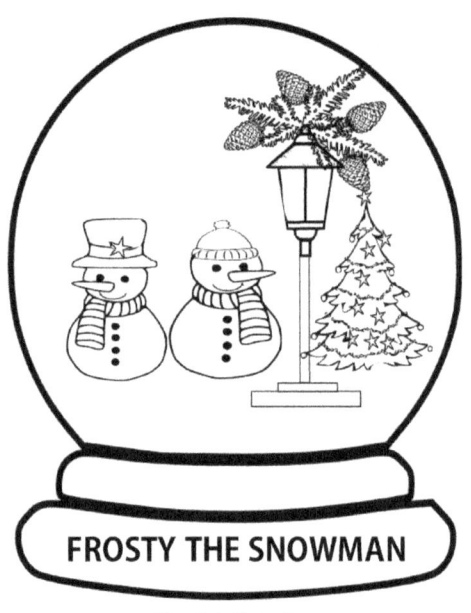

FROSTY THE SNOWMAN

Snow globe page 32

Aldona Design Therapeutic
Colouring book

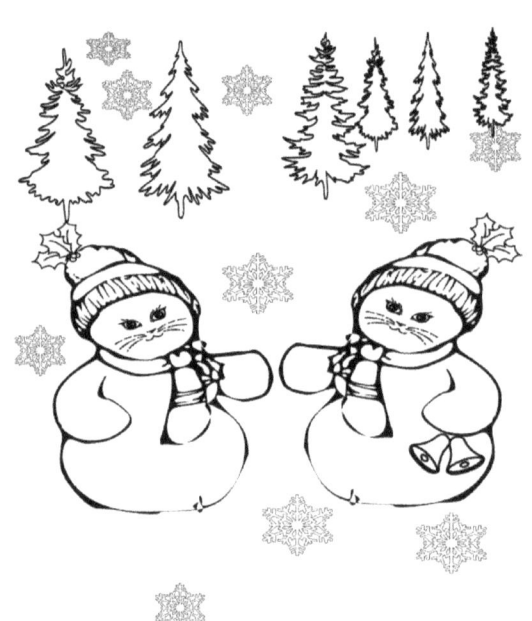

Cat snowman page 34

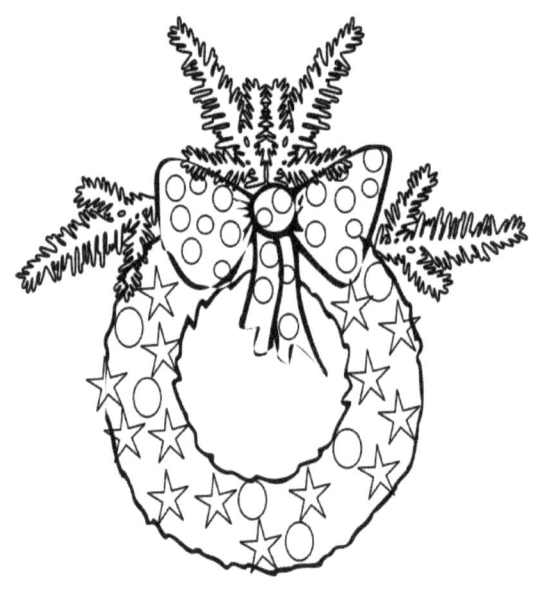

Wreath page 36

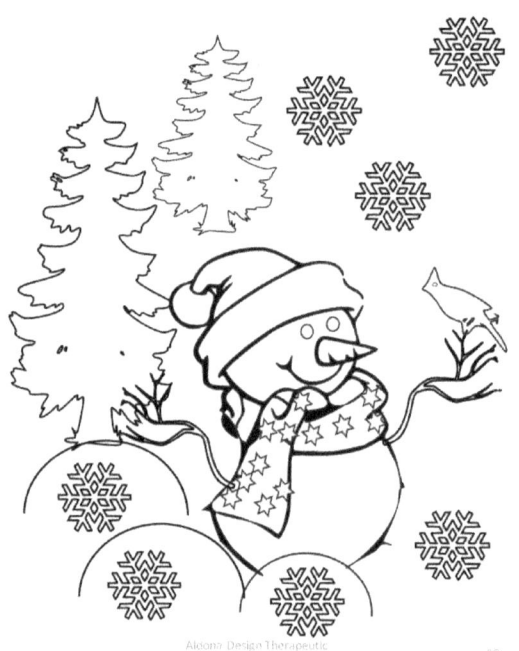

Snowman & Cardinal page 38

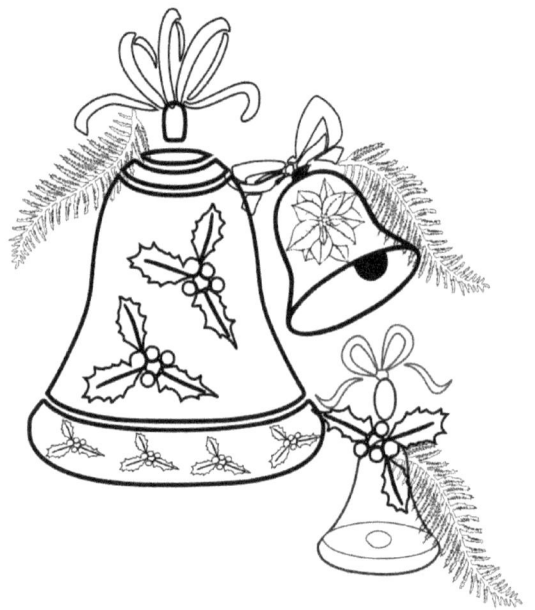

Bells page 30

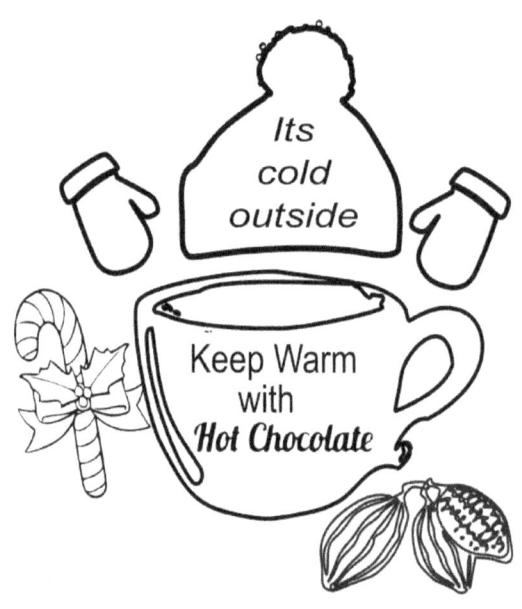

Its cold outside

Keep Warm
with
Hot Chocolate

Coco page 42

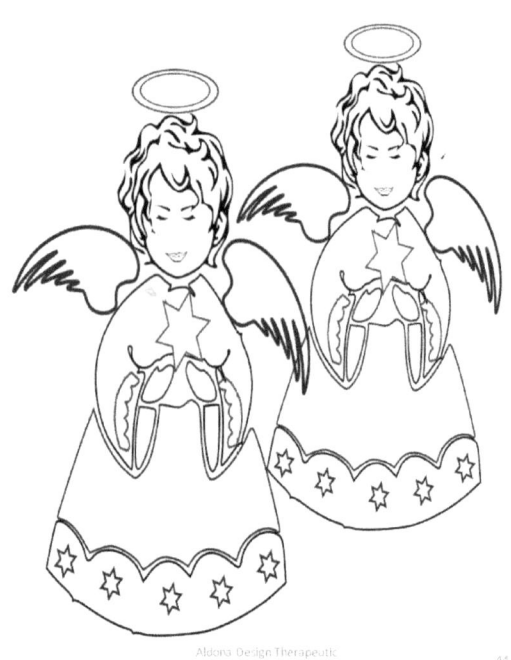

Angels page 44

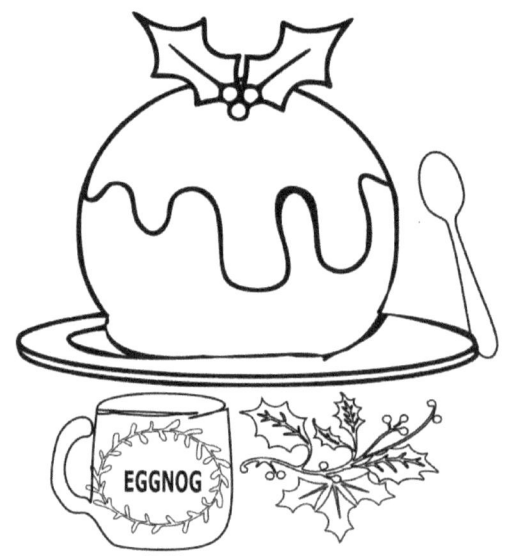

EGGNOG

Pudding & Eggnog page 46

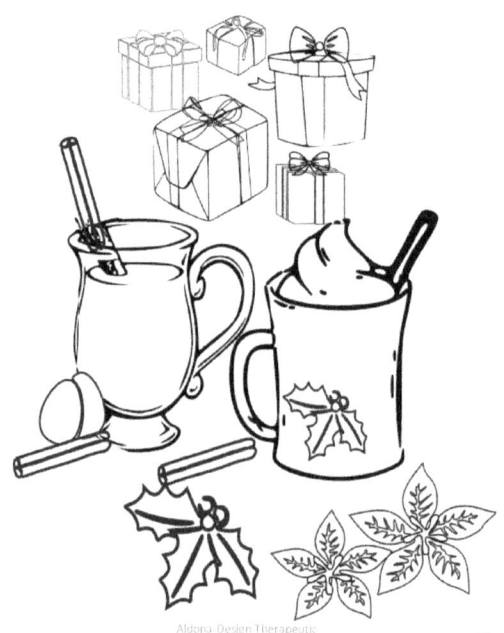

Coco & Eggnog & gifts page 48

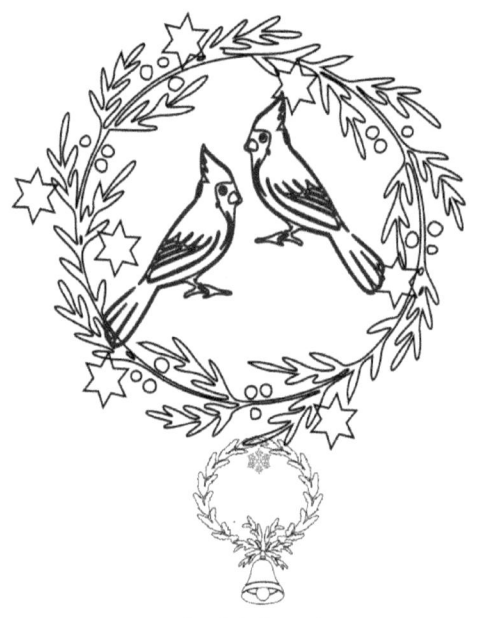

Cardinal & wreath page 50

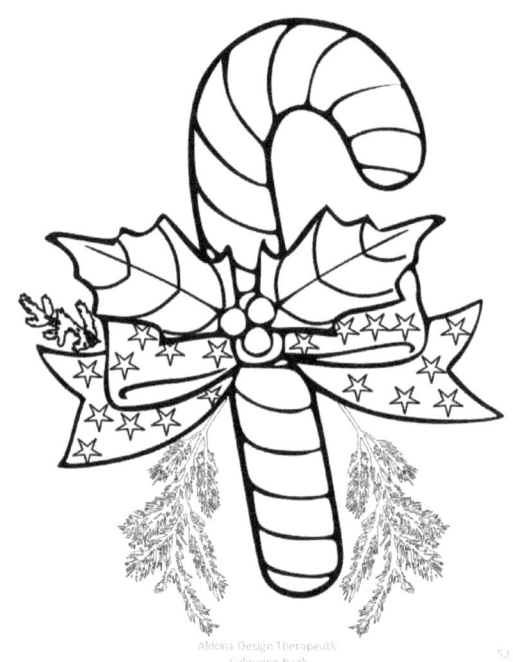

Candy cane page 52

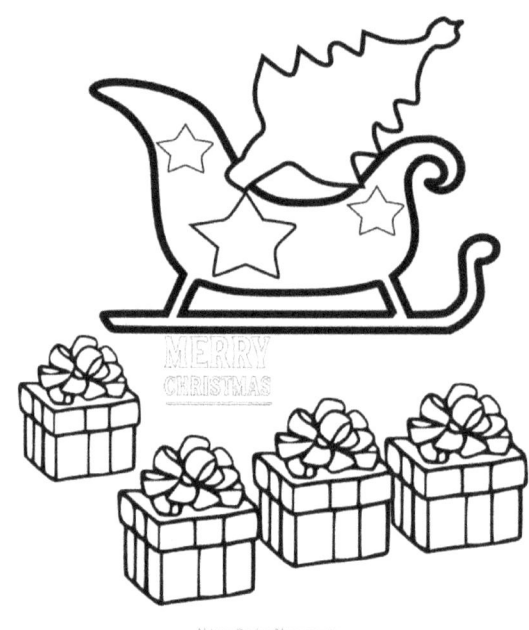

Sledge & gifts page 54

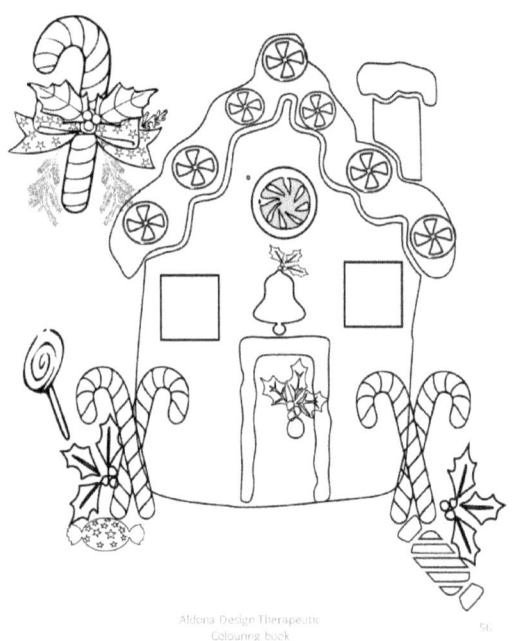

Gingerbread house page 56

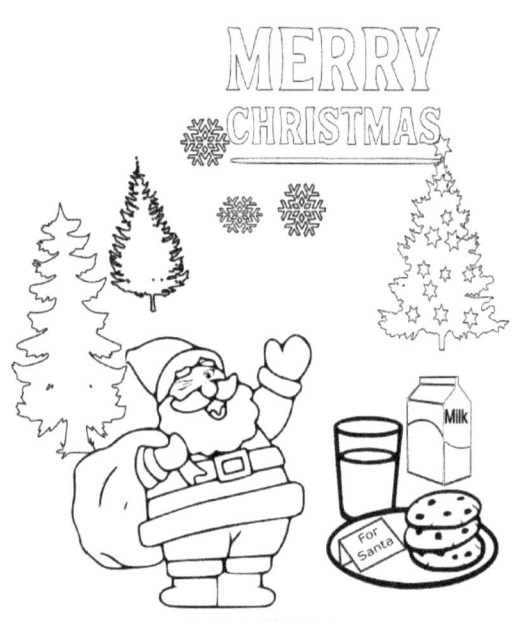

Santa & cookies & Milk page 58

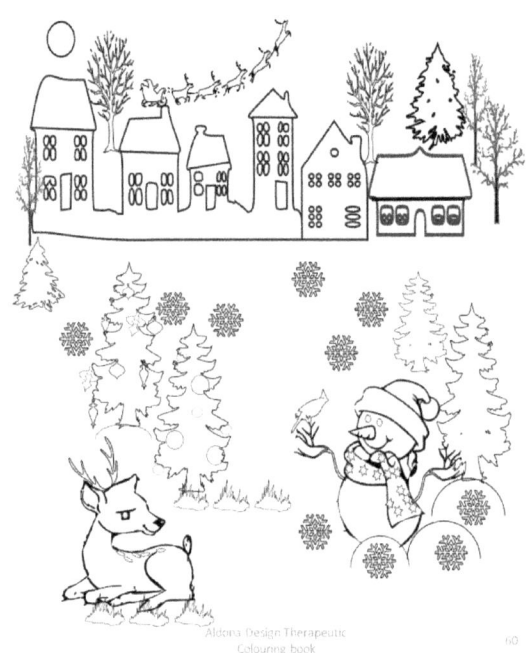

Winter City page 60

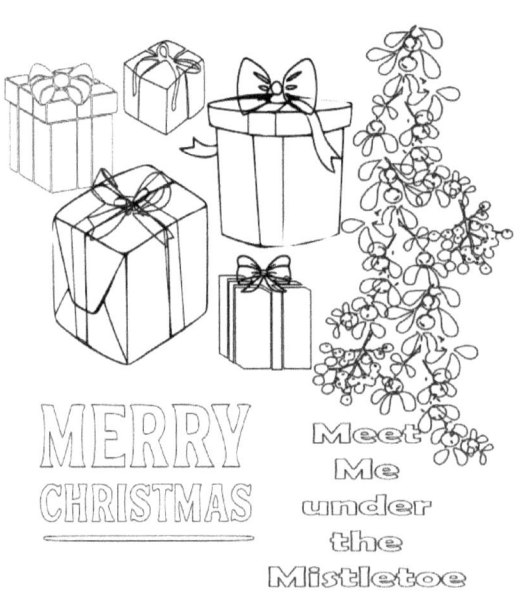

MERRY CHRISTMAS

Meet Me under the Mistletoe

Mistletoe & gifts page 62

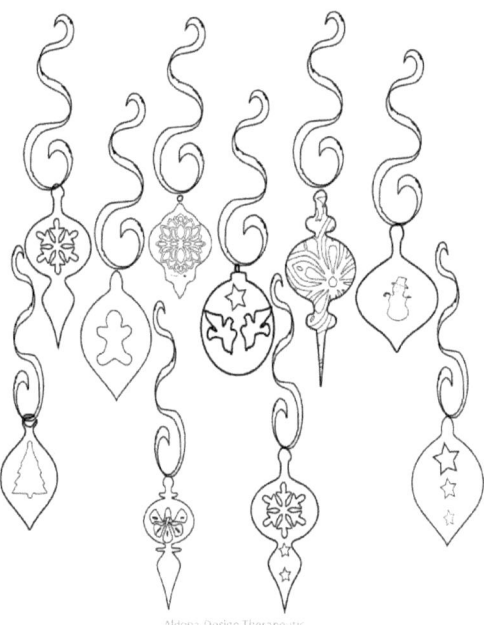

Hanging Ornaments page 64

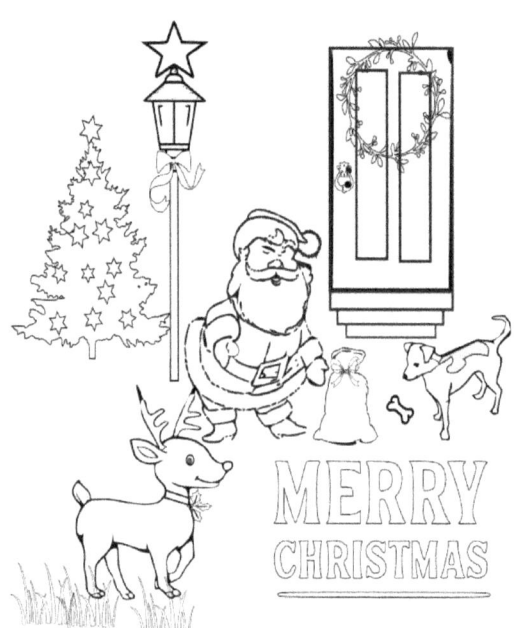

MERRY
CHRISTMAS

Santa with Dog page 66

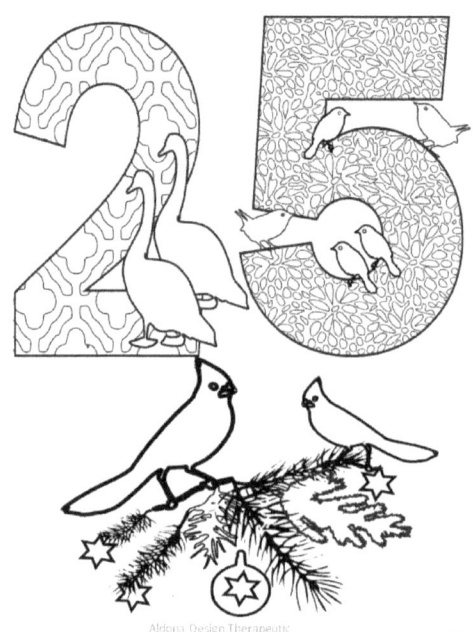

Cardinals on 25th page 68

Cardinals on 25th page 68

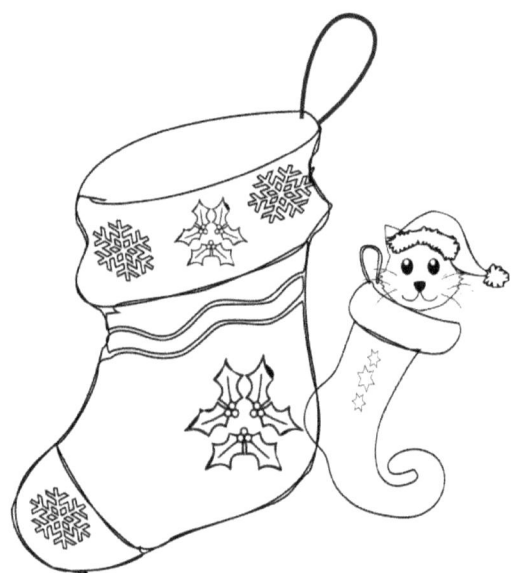

Stockings page 70

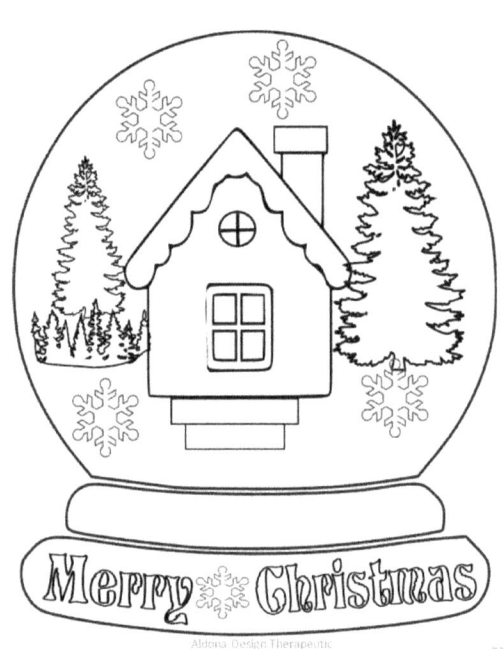

Snow Globe page 72

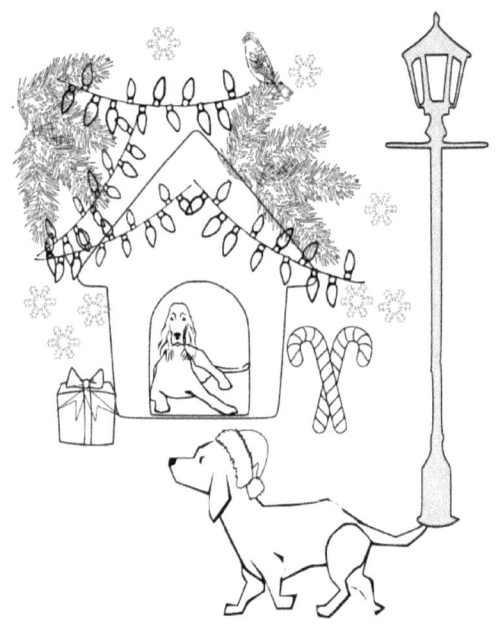

Doggies at Christmas page 4

Santa page 75

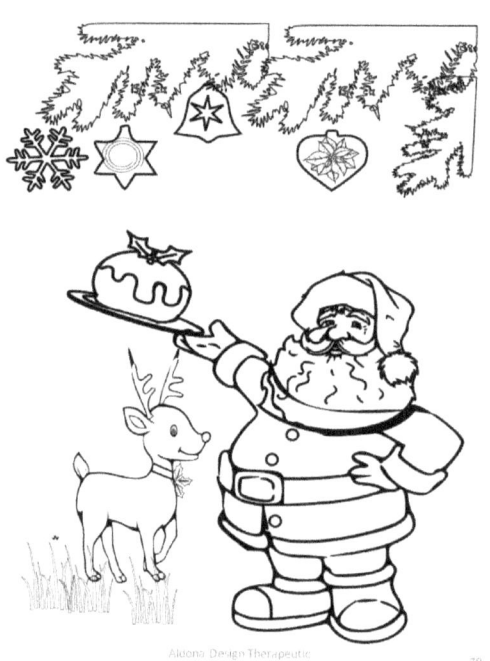

Santa & Pudding page 78

Ho ! Ho! Ho!

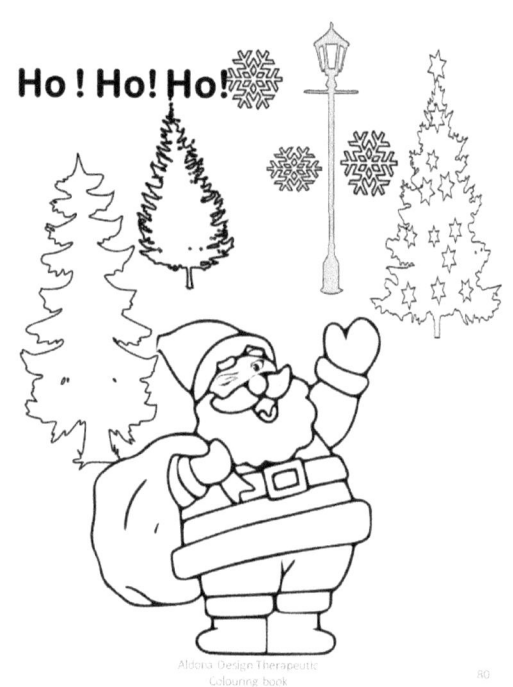

Santa is here page 80

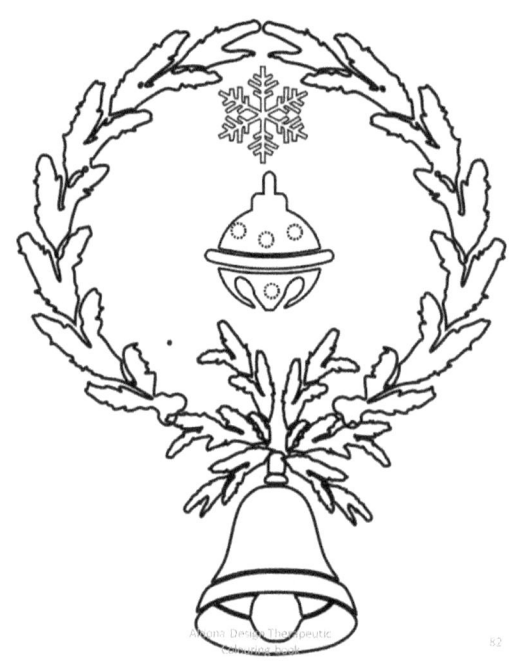

Wreaths & Bells page 82

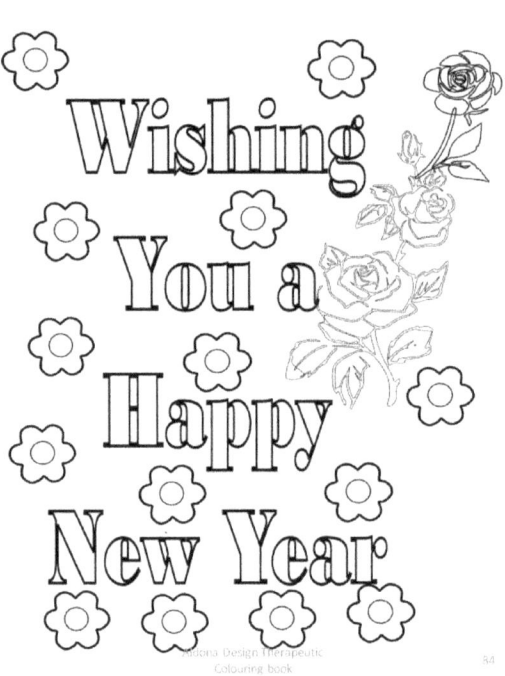

New Year Greetings page 84

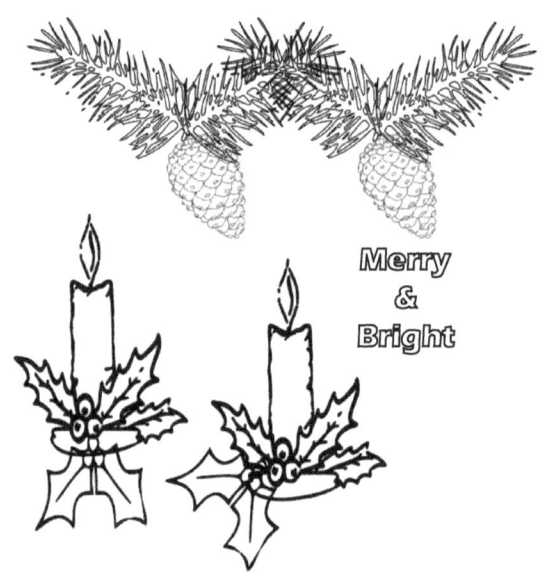

Merry
&
Bright

Candles & Streamers page 86

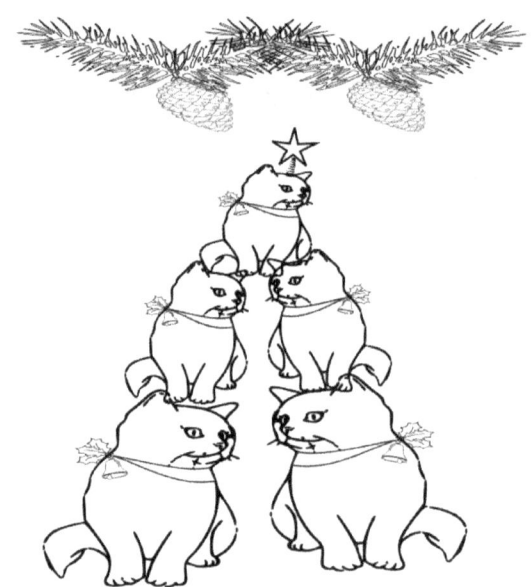

Christmas Cat tree page 88

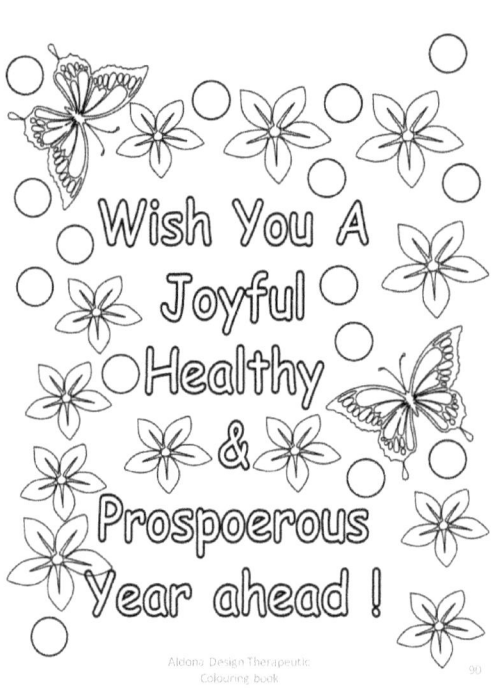

Wish You A
Joyful
Healthy
&
Prospoerous
Year ahead !

New Year Greetings page 90

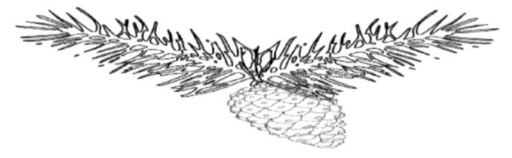

Snowman page 92

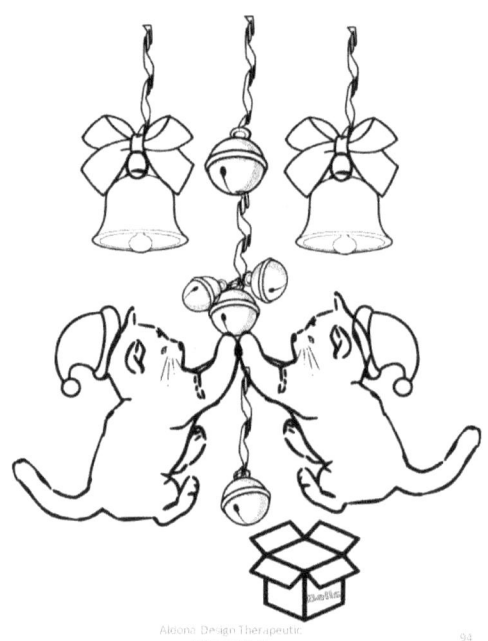

Cat & Bells page 94

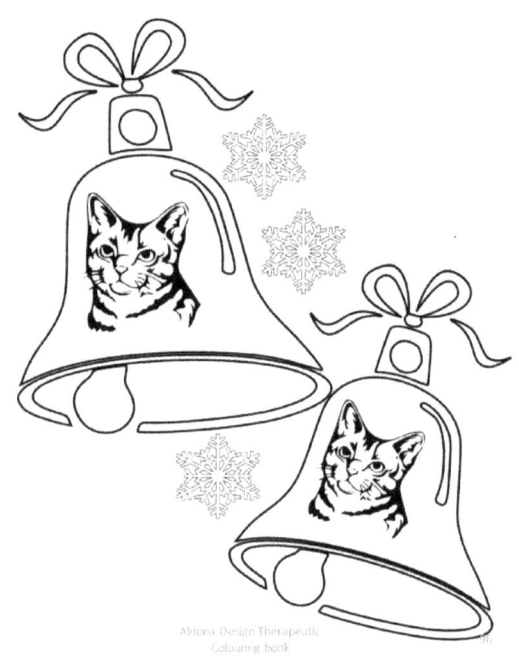

Cat on Bells page 96

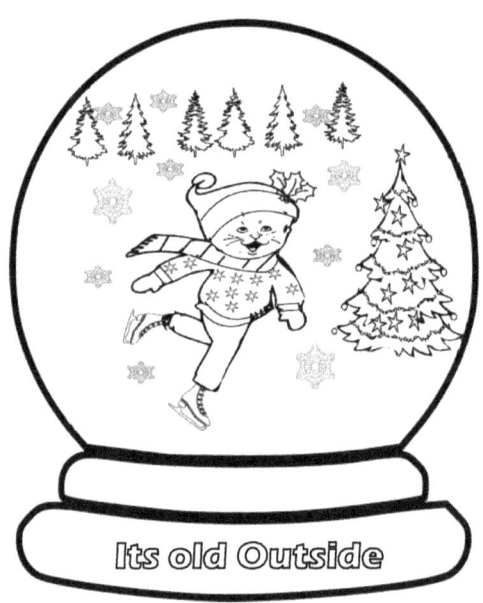

Its old Outside

Snow globe with cat skating page 94

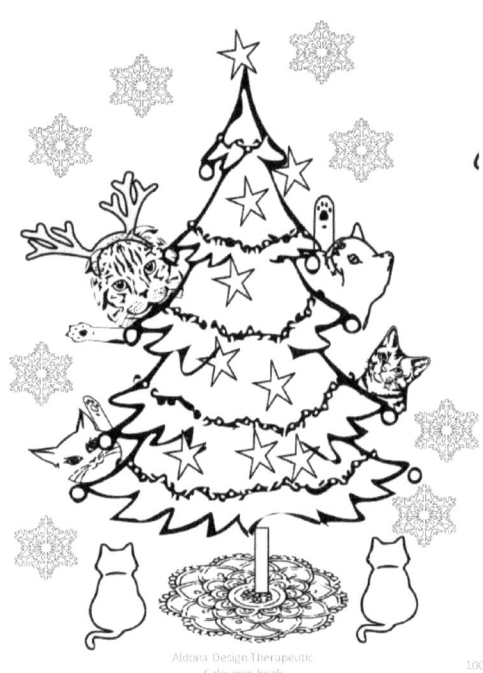

Cats & Tree page 100

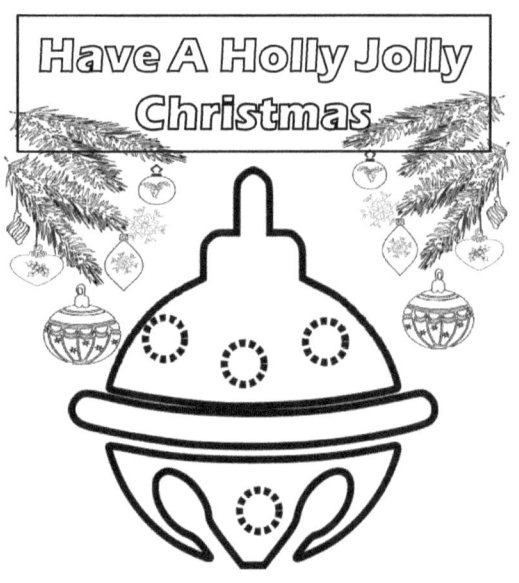

Greetings From Aldona Design page 102

Thank You for purchasing this book
We would appreciate your Opinion
About this book by leaving a
Review
 link follows
Email : **aldonadesign@gmail.com**
Instagram: https://www.instagram.com/aldona_design
Artwork:- http://www.redbubble.com/people/aldona
www.amazon.com/author/aldonadesign

<u>Colouring books for Adults with ISBN Number</u>
Therapeutic Colouring book: 100 one sided pages for adults
ISBN 1097666700
Therapeutic Colouring book II: **ISBN 1080663134**
Therapeutic Colouring Book III: **ISBN 1687402108**
(29 one sided Floral Patterns Adult Colouring Book)
Therapeutic Coloring book IV: **ISBN 1693086476**
(Adult Coloring Book of patterned Animals)
Therapeutic Colouring book V: **ISBN 1700582542**
(One sided page of 54 all year round Greetings for Adults)
Cute & Adorable Cat Colouring Book: **ISBN 1709770473**
(Best Adorable Colouring Gifts for all cat lovers, - Stress Relieving)
Therapeutic Christmas Colouring book VI
<u>Also Check out other Colour in Journals</u>
Calendar Journal: Blank Calendars & Tracking Goals, Habit, Moods,
Gratitude **ISBN 169259981X**
Gift tags: **ISBN 1690654244**
My Own Nail Art Design: **ISBN 1686035950**
<u>For Kids</u>
Christmas Colouring Book For Kids: **ISBN 1081432489**
Rock Painting & Design: Fun Activity book for all ages ISBN
170190909X
Just add the ISBN number to the end of the link below to
Make it easy to shop
https://www.amazon.com/gp/product/

www.ingramcontent.com/pod-product-compliance
Lightning Source LLC
Chambersburg PA
CBHW080842220526

45467CB00008B/2353